This book is dedicated to survivors and all those who work to assist them to achieve safety, nurturance and healing.

About the Safe & Together Institute

The Safe & Together Institute is a global leader in domestic violence-informed training and systems change. Our mission: Create a global network of professionals, organizations and communities working together to create domestic violence-informed child welfare and child-serving systems. We work everyday to change systems so they can be better allies to adult and child domestic violence survivors.

> *This book is not meant to replace official service, orders of protection or intervention orders, or calling the police in emergency situations. Nor does it constitute legal or mental health advice. It is also not intended to offer all the answers to very difficult or challenging situations. The user must be their own best guide for their actions.*

Concrete strategies.
Meaningful tools.
Real change.

PO BOX 745
CANTON, CONNECTICUT 06019
PHONE: 1 (860) 319-0966
WWW.SAFEANDTOGETHERINSTITUTE.COM

HOW TO BE AN ALLY

Contents

LETTER FROM THE FOUNDER	4
INTRODUCTION	5
DOMESTIC VIOLENCE ISN'T JUST ABOUT VIOLENCE, AND IT ISN'T JUST ABOUT THE ADULTS	6
BARRIERS TO IDENTIFYING A LOVED ONE IS BEING ABUSED	9
HOW DO DOMESTIC VIOLENCE AND COERCIVE CONTROL IMPACT ADULT AND CHILD SURVIVORS?	12
CODED DISCLOSURES: HOW SURVIVORS TELL YOU WITHOUT TELLING YOU	14
THE STEPS OF BEING AN EFFECTIVE ALLY	17
GETTING YOUR OWN HELP AND OTHER ISSUES	26
RESOURCES	31

"The concept behind this guide came from a survivor and was developed with input from other survivors. It represents their ideas about what they wanted and needed to hear from their loved ones."

**LETTER FROM DAVID MANDEL,
FOUNDER AND EXECTITIVE DIRECTOR
SAFE & TOGETHER INSTITUTE**

I'm proud to announce this ally guide for family and friends. For almost 15 years, the Safe & Together Institute has been training professionals all over the world to partner with domestic violence victims. This guide is our first resource targeted exclusively to people who are worried about a loved one experiencing abuse. Family and friends are often the first people to notice something is wrong, and the first people victims turn to for help. Unfortunately, despite loving and caring intentions, these conversations sometimes go awry. Learning your loved one is being abused can be scary. Your first instincts about how to respond may not be the right fit for her situation. Victims and their loved ones can walk away from these conversations feeling less than satisfied, and without any concrete progress toward safety.

The concept behind this guide came from a survivor and was developed with input from other survivors. It represents their ideas about what they wanted and needed to hear from their loved ones. The guide offers information about how to identify domestic violence. It explains how coercive control, even when there is no apparent violence, can be very harmful and dangerous. It offers specific concrete steps that family and friends can take to support a loved one who is being abused.

Family and friends are the most important resource that exists for domestic violence victims. I hope this ally guide assists them in providing more effective and loving support to their loved one who is being abused.

SECTION 1: Introduction

WHO IS THIS BOOK FOR?
This book is for friends and family who know a loved one experiencing domestic violence and coercive control and would like to know how best to support them. It is also for friends and family who have concerns about a loved one, but who aren't sure whether abuse is happening. (The terms "domestic violence" and "coercive control" are explained in detail in Section 2.)

WHY A BOOK FOR FAMILY AND FRIENDS?
Family and friends have a unique opportunity. Survivors often choose to seek their help and support before calling the police or engaging services. A positive first experience talking about the abuse can make the difference between safety and increased isolation and entrapment for a loved one. Knowing what to say and what not to say can help friends and family play the role they want to play: a source of support and safety for their loved one.

HOW SHOULD YOU USE IT?
This book is to be used to assist you in supporting a loved one who is navigating domestic violence and coercive control. It is not meant to replace professional assistance, court orders or involvement of law enforcement where appropriate. Rather, this book is designed to provide you with information, language and suggestions about how to respond to a very challenging, harmful and potentially dangerous situation.

WHAT IS AN ALLY?
An ally is someone who provides emotional support and practical assistance to another. To be an ally of someone who is experiencing domestic violence, you need to be able to listen, validate their experience, and, if possible and safe, provide tangible forms of support.

WHY DO WE SAY 'HE' FOR THOSE WHO CHOOSE VIOLENCE AND 'SHE' FOR THE SURVIVOR?
Throughout this guide, we refer to people who choose violence as "he" and survivors as "she." We want to explain the thinking behind this. First, we firmly acknowledge that both men and women can be violent and controlling and that domestic violence occurs in all types of relationships, including same-sex relationships. At the same time, it is important to recognize some key differences. Male against female violence and coercive control in heterosexual relationships is the most statistically common scenario. Men's violence toward women is more likely to be associated with physical injury, which is a proxy for fear and control. Men's violence is also more likely to be tied to wider patterns of coercive control. Unfortunately, most of us still live in communities where men are given more permission to be violent and to control other family members. Finally, since our work has been very focused on domestic violence and children, we've learned that ignoring the widely different expectations of men and women as parents is important and can make it harder for all of us to help survivors. That said, we hope the material in this guide will be useful across diverse situations. Throughout the guide, we will be offering additional information about domestic violence in diverse situations.

[Do you know someone who is being abused or you suspect is being abused? If you answer yes, this book is for you.]

DEFINITION: A survivor is someone who copes well with adversity. We use this term because you can assume your loved one has already developed strategies to help her and her children cope with their situation. We use the term 'victim' to underscore that your loved one is experiencing emotional or physical harm as result of the actions of another person. She is not to blame for the others' choices to hurt and control.

SECTION 2:
Domestic violence isn't just about violence, and it isn't just about the adults

DOMESTIC VIOLENCE IN DIVERSE SITUATIONS: When considering domestic abuse in diverse situations, examining these factors can help you identify the survivor in same-sex couples or the less frequent situation where a man is trapped in a coercively controlling relationship.

Most people think of domestic violence as physical violence like punching, kicking or slapping. They would be right, but limited, in their understanding. Physical violence doesn't need to happen every day or ever for domestic violence to be a problem.

It's most useful to understand domestic violence as a series of behaviors that can make other family members feel:

- less safe
- limited in their choices
- less satisfaction with their life
- less connected with others
- less joy
- fearful and traumatized

Some of these behaviors, like sexual assault, threats of violence or strangulation can lead to arrest. Many behaviors associated with domestic violence do not lead to arrest. Name-calling, put-downs, control over money, interfering with relationships, undercutting another's parenting, checking texts, monitoring calls and controlling others' movements are common behaviors. In more and more countries, this pattern of behaviors is being referred to as "coercive control."

> *Do you have a loved one who has started acting very differently since they got into a relationship? Are they less available? Do they seem less happy? Do they seem to be less open in how they speak to you? These may be signs of abuse.*

The range of behaviors associated with domestic violence and coercive control is so wide it is hard to make a full list. Here are some examples of behaviors that might give you a sense of what to look for:

- Demonstrations of violence against inanimate objects like punching walls, hurting pets or threatening violence against strangers
- Threats of self-harm, like committing suicide, if the other person ever left or reported them
- Threatening to take children by calling child protection or threatening court action
- Violence when drinking or using other drugs
- Limiting the ability of the survivor to work or access transportation, education, family, friends, the internet and other forms of communication
- Pressuring someone to have sex when they don't want to
- Demanding the other person comply with whims, needs, desires and demands
- Blaming the other person for their discomfort with the world, themselves, their insecurities or their anger
- Accusing their partner of infidelity
- Creating an unpredictable environment where no one knows what response to expect
- Ruling by threat, chaos, anger, verbal abuse, heavy-handed 'punishment' meant to frighten or destroy others' sense of safety or security

Each of these behaviors by themselves can be harmful. But when they are combined together, especially with the presence or threat of physical violence, they can have a devastating effect on the day-to-day quality of life for family members. And when someone has vulnerabilities, it may not take a lot for them to feel trapped. For example, someone who has significant health issues may not feel like they can leave an abusive relationship and make it on their own.

DOMESTIC VIOLENCE IN DIVERSE SITUATIONS: Threats and acts of control can be very targeted in a specific population. For example, someone may leverage underlying fears of transphobic system responses when threatening to take children away from a trans-parent.

DOMESTIC VIOLENCE IN DIVERSE SITUATIONS: Wider cultural patterns of racism and oppression can fuel entrapment. If your loved one is part of a vulnerable or oppressed group, their partner may be leveraging their situation to gain more control. For example, undocumented immigrants' fears of deportation may give the person choosing violence more freedom to be abusive without fear that the survivor will call law enforcement.

A PERSON WHO CHOOSES VIOLENCE DOESN'T JUST TARGET THEIR PARTNER

Domestic violence and child abuse can be connected through multiple pathways. The impact on children may start early with forcing someone to have a child or violence during pregnancy. A parent who chooses to engage in coercive control is almost always engaging in forms of emotional child neglect and abuse.

> **!** If you are aware of these kinds of behaviors being done against a loved one, there may be ways you can help them. Keep reading!

> **DOMESTIC VIOLENCE IN DIVERSE SITUATIONS:** Children with physical, mental or emotional limitations are likely to be more vulnerable to abuse and neglect. If your loved one has a child with special needs, they may feel even more trapped.

Sometimes there is also physical neglect and abuse. And while not as common as other forms of child abuse and neglect, sometimes a person who uses coercive control also may be sexually abusing their children.

Like with coercive control, the full list of actions that harm children is so wide that it is difficult to make a complete list. Here are some examples that might give you a sense of what to look for:

- Witnessing physical violence or threats of violence against a family member
- Witnessing physical violence or threats of violence against strangers
- Physical abuse of children
- Name-calling or other humiliating behavior toward the children
- Constant criticism and belittling
- Driving dangerously with children in the car
- Exposing children to pornography
- Leaving children in unsupervised or unsafe situations
- Undercutting the other parent's rules
- Attacking the other person's parenting
- Pitting different family members against each other
- Disrupting daily routines, housing and schooling through the use of violence
- Interfering with children getting the physical or emotional health support they need

These types of actions can have profound implications for children's day-to-day life especially when violence forces the children to move, change schools, and lose access to family and friends.

> **!** **Action:** If you know a young person who is growing up in a household with violence, you can make a difference in their life by being a safe person who listens and cares. Be that someone!

SECTION 3:
Barriers to identifying a loved one is being abused

DON'T ALL COUPLES ARGUE AND HAVE FIGHTS?

Yes, disagreements are common in relationships. Coercive control is different than "normal" couple problems. Most couples argue and struggle with shared decision-making without violence, threats or actions that crush the other person's sense of self. Raising your voice during a fight doesn't mean that others will be afraid or feel controlled. We are talking about patterns of behaviors that make others feel smaller, afraid for their safety, and attack their sense of self. Coercive control is a systematic attack on another person's freedom and ability to control their own life.

> DOMESTIC VIOLENCE IN DIVERSE SITUATIONS: If your loved one and her partner have both been arrested for domestic violence, do not assume they both have a problem with violence. Often, when someone attempts to use violence to protect themselves, that person can be arrested alone or with the abusive partner.

 **Action:** Some families yell while they argue, and nobody is afraid. In other families, quiet arguments can be very scary when backed up by unspoken threats of violence. Your loved one's situation of abuse may not look scary from the outside but may actually be very dangerous. Do not assume!

IS DOMESTIC VIOLENCE EASY TO SPOT?

Sometimes yes. Sometimes no. In some instances, domestic violence is easy to identify because we may witness it right in front of our eyes. Or the adult or child survivors may directly disclose it to us. Or we may see obvious signs like a black eye or an arrest. At the same time, it's useful to understand the barriers to identifying it. Here are some:

Many people who choose to be violent act differently around family members, friends and work colleagues. In fact, they might be charming, polite and helpful to others.

In many cultures and communities, there is a tendency to allow families to deal with their own problems, giving them space and privacy to navigate their own problems as a couple or a family. This makes a lot of sense except when the health and safety of family members are in jeopardy. Domestic violence and coercive control are not "normal" couple or family problems.

Domestic violence and coercive control may hide behind the mask of religion, deeply held beliefs or other mainstream ideas or behaviors. For example, some people who choose to be violent use religion to justify their abuse. A decision to home school children may be part of an attempt to control the lives of family members and keep adult and child survivors limited in their contact with the outside world. In communities and cultures which have a heavy emphasis on male-dominated family structures, it can be very difficult to identify the presence of domestic violence and coercive control.

> **Action:** Hidden domestic violence may make it harder to believe disclosures about coercive control and violence, and can increase a survivor's sense of isolation. It can also make her feel "crazy" because nobody else is seeing these behaviors. It may add to her sense of shame and guilt. If he only acts this way toward his partner, it becomes easier for him to tell her it's her fault. Believe survivors' disclosures!

WILL DOMESTIC VIOLENCE SURVIVORS ALWAYS IMMEDIATELY LABEL WHAT THEY ARE EXPERIENCING AS ABUSE?

No. For many survivors, labeling the behaviors they are experiencing as abuse is a process. They may struggle to admit that they've allowed someone else to gain control over their lives. They may struggle to sort out cultural messages about things like love, marriage and jealousy. Their love for the person who chooses violence may make it hard to label them an "abuser" or "perpetrator." They associate the terms "domestic violence" or "victim" with something that happens to "other people." If you want to support your loved one, you will be patient with their process of understanding what is happening to them.

CAN DOMESTIC VIOLENCE HAPPEN AFTER A COUPLE IS SEPARATED OR DIVORCED?

Yes, it can. In fact, post-separation, a person who chooses to use coercive control may escalate and become more dangerous because he feels like he is losing control over his partner and the situation. Post-separation tactics are attempts to pressure someone to return to them or punish them for leaving by attempting to control their parenting, relationships and life choices. These behaviors can include:

> HOW DOES COERCIVE CONTROL WORK? Some survivors will decide not to pursue child support, even when legally entitled to it, in order to avoid escalating violence or control. Being an ally to your loved one means understanding how the person who has chosen violence continues to shape her choices even after separation. Telling her that "her children deserve child support and she should fight for it!" may not be what she needs to hear. Instead, listen to her hopes and fears and try to help her make the best decision for her situation.

> Do not assume that because your loved one left their partner that she and her children are safe, or that life is automatically easier. This may be the period they need the most support. Be that support person!

- using the courts or threats of litigation to control his ex-partner
- using the children as a weapon to get back at his ex-partner
- financially abusing an ex-partner by refusing to pay child support or stop working to avoid payments
- threatening or actually calling child protection to make false reports
- spreading rumors
- stalking both in real life and online
- violating court orders
- threatening to take the children
- abusing the children during visits
- emotionally manipulating the children

ARE DOMESTIC VIOLENCE AND COERCIVE CONTROL THE SAME AS HAVING A "TEMPER" PROBLEM?

Thinking of domestic violence and coercive control as just being a "temper problem" or an "anger management" issue is a common mistake. Defining it as a temper problem misses the entire point of the impact it has on other people, how much of the controlling behavior happens when someone is not angry, and blinds us to the more subtle dynamics of control. The person who chooses violence is often not acting violently toward their boss at work or other people outside the family. This shows us that no matter what their feelings, this person is still capable of choosing not to be violent when they wish.

 Action: While your loved one may describe their partner as having a "temper," being an ally means asking questions about what "having a temper" means and how much control and fear are being created through that "temper." Don't assume having a temper is normal!

SECTION 4:
How do domestic violence and coercive control impact adult and child survivors?

Using domestic violence and coercive control is both a relationship and a parenting choice that impacts the health, well-being and development of children. It weakens the family and leaves children vulnerable to future abuse by partners or to adopting abusive behaviors themselves.

A person who chooses violence or coercive control makes choices that hurt their loved ones in multiple areas. These areas include:

- School
- Work
- Housing
- Mental Health
- Physical Health
- Substance Use
- Relationships
- Parenting

Some of the effects are short term and immediate, like physical injuries from an assault. Others are longer-term and chronic, like depression. Some effects, like losing a job, can ripple through the entire family for a long time. Children who are afraid for their parent's safety will often experience anxiety, depression, behavioral issues, and as they get older engage in risky behaviors like substance abuse, suicidal attempts, eating disorders or involvement with gangs. Infants and young children may experience developmental delays and trouble sleeping, eating or being easily soothed.

 **Action:** Remember that changes in a loved one's life may not be the result of their choices but the choices of the person who uses violence. Avoid blaming them for their partner's choices!

WHAT SYMPTOMS OF ABUSE SHOULD I BE LOOKING FOR?

Some adult and children survivors experience abuse severe enough that they have significant physical and emotional symptoms. Here are some examples of what you may expect to see in survivors:

- Anxiety
- Chronic health issues including autoimmune disorders
- Depression
- Substance abuse
- Mental health disorders
- Fear
- Confusion
- A sense of hopelessness
- Inability to concentrate
- Physical limitations like hearing loss due to blows to the head
- Self-harm, cutting
- Isolation
- Inability to cope or organize themselves or their children
- Suicidal thoughts and attempts
- Perfectionism
- Overachievement

Many of these are the natural reactions of a body trying to cope with trauma and ongoing harm. Others are common forms of coping or forms of resistance to the abuse.

> **DOMESTIC VIOLENCE IN DIVERSE SITUATIONS:** If you are worried a male loved one or loved one in a same-sex relationship is being abused, you want to look for the same pattern of coercive control and entrapment. Here are some questions to consider:
> » Is your loved one scared of being severely hurt or killed by their partner's violence?
> » Does your loved one's partner use words and actions to diminish her partner's room to maneuver, e.g., has your loved one's life gotten smaller?
> » What consequence will your loved one face if he or she stands up for themselves, tells others, or tries to leave or break the "rules"? How difficult will the partner make your loved one's life?

WHAT OTHER SIGNS AND SYMPTOMS SHOULD I BE LOOKING FOR?

In addition to physical and emotional health symptoms, there are other signs that might indicate abuse is going on behind closed doors. This list will give you an idea of some things to look for:

- Frequent moves
- Sudden or repeated loss of jobs for either partner
- Children missing days at school
- Excessive or extreme disrespect of a parent or other authority figure
- Distancing oneself from relatives and friends
- Never letting your loved one be alone with other people
- Absence from social events including family gatherings
- The partner showing up unexpectedly
- Repeated phone calls from the partner while your loved one is visiting
- Your loved one giving up on her dreams and plans
- Your loved one becomes marginalized in their own household
- Your loved one's partner handling all the communications with others

While domestic violence and coercive control are not the only causes of these signs, it is important to keep them in mind as possible reasons for what you are seeing.

[
Do you have a loved one who is a different person when their partner is around? This may be a sign of control issues. Reach out to them using some of the ideas in this book to check if they are okay.
]

SECTION 5: Coded Disclosures: How survivors tell you without telling you

Often survivors signal to us indirectly that they are being abused or controlled. In some instances, they are consciously testing the waters by giving hints. In other instances, they are trying to explain or justify their partners' behavior to themselves and to you. It is very important to listen for their "coded" phrases and learn how to follow up in a useful and supportive way.

Here are some common phrases which may be 'code' that your loved one is being abused or coercively controlled:

- He doesn't like it when...
- He gets angry a lot...
- He pops off...
- He loses it...
- He likes things a particular way or else...
- He is in charge of the money
- He watches everything I spend and do
- We aren't allowed to/ He won't let me...
- I often feel crazy when I try to talk to him about his behaviors and how they affect me and the kids

- He has a bad/short temper
- He is controlling
- He doesn't like it when I do...
- He wants things 'just so'
- He doesn't like it when the children...
- I have to walk on eggshells...
- He is hard on the kids
- He is a rough disciplinarian
- He punishes me with silence
- He hurts me sometimes but doesn't mean to

HOW NOT TO RESPOND TO DISCLOSURES

How we respond to these disclosures is so important. A positive response will help your loved one open up more and feel supported. A negative response may shut them down and make them feel more isolated. Here is a partial list of certain types of responses to avoid:

- Asking her what she did to provoke it
- Telling her to comply with his demands in order to keep the peace
- Blaming her for being in the relationship or 'choosing' the relationship
- Telling her that men are just naturally "like that"
- Telling her God wants her to make the marriage work
- Telling her that she is smarter than that and she just needs to leave
- Telling her that disclosure will hurt your community
- Telling her that talking about it will hurt her partner
- Saying, "At least he isn't hitting you every day"
- Telling her that your own partner is abusive and it's just something you deal with
- Trying to guilt her or force her into actions which you believe will be protective
- Saying, "You should be grateful because you have a man who works and comes home every night"
- Asking her what is wrong with her
- Telling her that she is putting their kids at risk
- Telling her to forgive or 'turn the other cheek'
- Telling her it's a woman's job to keep the peace in the home

DOMESTIC VIOLENCE IN DIVERSE SITUATIONS: In communities that have experienced oppression, and distrust formal systems, there can be a strong message of "do not air our dirty laundry to others." This is an understandable attitude but it can lead to feelings of greater entrapment. It is important to communicate to your loved one that she deserves safety and that you support her decisions such as calling the police or talking about the abuse.

What these responses have in common is that they make the survivor responsible for their partner's behavior, it normalizes abuse, or it uses social and emotional pressure to shut down the disclosure.

Action: It can be easy to compare situations. Just because someone doesn't disclose physical violence, do not assume the situation isn't harmful or dangerous. When situations do not involve current physical violence, your listening and being supportive can really help the person figure out what she needs to do!

HOW TO RESPOND TO DISCLOSURES

A constructive and positive response to your loved one's disclosure can make all the difference. You have two different pathways of response: direct and indirect. Use the less direct when you want to approach the topic more slowly. The more direct approach is when you think it would be useful to dive right in. Here are some examples of each type:

LESS DIRECT:

- That sounds like it must make things harder for you.
- Does that work for you?
- What is he "popping off" about?
- Does he understand how he's treating you is bad for you and the kids?
- In my relationship, we work to make decisions together.
- God wants us to feel like we matter.
- It must be hard to figure out what you can spend on groceries and the children when he doesn't let you know how much is in the bank.
- It sounds like he wants you to do things his way even when he isn't living with you.

MORE DIRECT:

- When you say, he gets "angry" what does that mean?
- What does it look like when he...?
- What does he do or say when that happens?
- Are you afraid when he...?
- Has he done anything threatening or joked about harming you or the children?
- What does he do that makes you afraid?
- What do you think he would do if you left?
- How do you think he would respond if you did (something he doesn't like)?
- What are you afraid of the most?

These conversations may not be straightforward. Be patient and go slow. Your loved one may be confused about her responsibility for what is going on. It is not uncommon to see survivors disclose and then retract their disclosures by saying that the abuse 'isn't that bad', or they were simply 'overreacting'. This is a self-protective mechanism. It may be a sign the victim does not yet feel that they are safe enough to disclose. The person choosing violence may have created an environment of control through guilting the victim by threats of self-harm, by exploiting fears of repression or potential harm to him by law enforcement, or by telling her that things will be worse for her and the children if she reports him. Your loved one may be afraid of losing her financial well-being, her family stability, her housing or resources for the children. Vulnerabilities, particularly among populations that already experience racism or oppression, are real and may increase the victim's reluctance to talk.

Action: Listen and don't tell your loved one how to act! Listening and providing support is one of the best ways you can help!

WWW.SAFEANDTOGETHERINSTITUTE.COM

SECTION 6:
The Steps of Being an Effective Ally

Being an ally to a loved one who is being abused can literally make the difference between life and death. It can also be something that helps your loved one understand there is help, and make sense of the situation they are in. By using the following ally behaviors, you can make a difference.

Ally Behavior #1: Tell her that only the person who is choosing violence is responsible for those behaviors and their consequences. She is not causing or provoking those behaviors.
Ally Behavior #2: Learn more about what is being done to her.
Ally Behavior #3: Validate all the things she is doing right for herself and her children.
Ally Behavior #4: Offer practical support.

ALLY BEHAVIOR #1: TELL HER THAT ONLY THE PERSON WHO IS CHOOSING VIOLENCE IS RESPONSIBLE FOR THOSE BEHAVIORS, AND THEIR CONSEQUENCES. SHE IS NOT CAUSING OR PROVOKING THOSE BEHAVIORS.

The Why: People who choose violence and control try to maintain that control by blaming the person(s) who are the target(s) of those behaviors. This is a form of manipulation and mind-control. When you tell the survivor that the abuse is not their fault, it can help them feel safer talking to you about what is going on, and reduce the amount of control the other person has over their thoughts and feelings.

The How: Explicitly tell the survivor that her partner's control and violence is not her fault and that the person choosing coercive control and violence is 100% responsible for their own behavior and their consequences. Here are some examples of what to say:

> His choices to harm you and the children are his own

> He is choosing to do things which hurt you and the children

> There is nothing you did to deserve this

- *I am here for you.*
- *No one should be treated this way.*
- *His choices to harm you and the children are his own.*
- *There is nothing you did to deserve this.*
- *You and the children deserve to be safe and nurtured.*
- *That (name the specific behavior) is abusive and not nurturing; it is destructive and harmful.*
- *That is not the action of someone who is loving.*
- *Abusing you is a harmful parenting choice.*
- *You are not crazy to want to be safe and treated with respect.*
- *You did nothing to provoke this, his behaviors are his choice.*
- *It is not ok for him to treat you that way.*
- *Of course, you are scared/hurt/confused/angry; that is understandable considering his behaviors.*
- *Even if you've made mistakes (examples: used drugs, cheated on him), he has no right to abuse you.*

You cannot say these things too often. Survivors often carry a tremendous amount of guilt and shame and a sense of responsibility for what is happening.

> **DOMESTIC VIOLENCE IN DIVERSE SITUATIONS:** Financial control can happen at all levels of society. It can take the form of running up credit card debt in your loved one's name or using money as a form of manipulation or bribery. Bringing groceries over after a separation, buying the children expensive toys or threatening not to pay child support can all be forms of guilt, emotional manipulation, and using the children to control your loved one.

ALLY BEHAVIOR #2: LEARN MORE ABOUT WHAT IS BEING DONE TO HER.

The Why: There is often much more to the pattern of abusive behavior than meets the eye. When you ask questions about what the abuse looks like, you are a) continuing to validate your loved one's experiences, b) gaining a deeper understanding of her situation, and c) gathering information that might help you help her.

The How: Ask specifics about the behaviors of the person choosing to be violent or use coercive control. You can be both direct and sensitive. Some survivors are ready to talk and others may need more patience. She may feel humiliation and shame talking about what has been done to her. Be loving and supportive as you listen and ask questions. Follow her lead.

You are listening and asking about the following:
- The impact that those behaviors have had on her, her children and the functioning of their family
- Patterns of behavior that may be putting her in serious danger
- How the person choosing violence has responded to interventions or efforts to get help in the past

> You and the children deserve to be safe and nurtured

> No one should be treated this way

> You are not crazy to want to be safe and treated with respect

1. ***Learn the person who is choosing violence's coercively controlling actions directed at your loved one and her children.***

The following are some lists of behaviors that can help you talk to your loved one about what she is experiencing. The major areas of coercive control include:

- Physical violence
- Sexual violence
- Physical and non-physical threats like "If you leave me, I'll take the children from you"
- Intimidating behavior like punching walls
- Control over finances
- Emotional and sexual abuse
- Undermining the other person's parenting
- Attacking the relationship between family members
- Sabotaging outside relationships
- Sabotaging employment or education
- Using children as weapons against the other person

Every situation is different. If you hear things that are difficult or hard to hear, try to keep an even response. Your loved one is assessing you to see how you respond. If it appears you are being traumatized or overwhelmed by what she is sharing, she may shut down. At the same time, it is okay to convey the seriousness of what she is talking about and express your concern or worry for her and her children.

2. ***Learn about the impact that those behaviors have had on her, her children and the functioning of their family (see page 12-13 for impacts).***

As your loved one shares with you about her situation, listen for how these behaviors have impacted her day-to-day life, the children's life and the overall functioning of the family. People who choose to use violence can traumatize other family members - including children - and make daily functioning harder, and cause major disruptions to the family, like forcing them to move.

Here are some examples of what you can say to your loved one when she tells you about the impact. Statements like these can help her feel validated.

- "It sounds like your daughter still wants to sleep in the same bed as you because he's made her afraid that something bad will happen to you."
- "It sounds like his yelling is making your son's stutter worse."
- "I'm sorry. I didn't realize all that moving around you did was because he kept getting you evicted from your apartment or he forced you to move."
- "I just thought you were pissed off at me. I'm sorry I didn't realize he was forcing you to take his side against us."
- "I was confused when you dropped out of school because you were so excited about getting a degree. I didn't realize he was creating so much trouble at home that you didn't feel okay about leaving the kids with him."
- "Sounds like he doesn't care if he makes bedtime for the kids harder for you."
- "I never liked the way the children talked to you. I always thought you should be tougher on them. I never realized he was teaching them to talk to you that way."

> DOMESTIC VIOLENCE IN DIVERSE SITUATIONS: Your loved one has a right to want to keep living in their own home or remain connected to the land of their tribe or nation. Having to choose between safety and leaving one's home, land and community is unfair. Validate her anger at the unfairness and, at the same time, help her plan for choices that will improve the safety of her and her children. Help her look for ways to stay connected to things that are important to her and also improve safety.

3. **Look for patterns of behavior that may be putting her in serious danger.**

Some situations are very scary and dangerous. It is hard to predict how far any situation will escalate but it is important to understand when your loved one might be in danger of serious injury or even death. Some survivors will tell you outright, "I'm worried he's going to kill me." Take those statements very seriously. Some survivors need help piecing together signs. In order to help your loved one, especially if they are thinking about leaving the relationship, you need to know some potential indicators of higher levels of danger.

> *Leaving or getting help may actually escalate the danger. Escalating erratic behavior or paranoia, depression, increased substance use can be warning signs of increased danger.*

Prior behaviors that may be associated with higher levels of danger to your loved ones include:

- Strangulation attempts
- Use of weapons or assaults that create severe injury
- Alcohol or drug use
- Threats of homicide to her and/or the children
- Threats of suicide
- Extreme jealousy including stalking
- Extensive control over day-to-day activities
- Sexual assault
- Physical violence during pregnancy
- History of violence toward others outside the family

If you hear your loved one talk about these factors, you can tell her you're really worried about her safety. Any plans for helping her need to account for her partner's potential escalation in danger to her, the children and others.

> **!** Action: Planning for leaving is complicated and may take time, especially if children are involved. In her decision making, your loved one is also probably considering financial factors like work and insurance, stability issues like housing and school, and other factors like closeness to family. She's likely to be thinking both short term and long term. Listening to her can help her figure out her best options.

- *Of course, you are scared/hurt/confused/angry; that is understandable considering his behaviors*
- *You did nothing to provoke this, his behaviors are his choice*
- *Abusing you is a parenting choice*

4. How has the person choosing violence responded to interventions or efforts to get help in the past?

Each person who has chosen violence will react differently to outside interventions. Some will move on to another relationship. Others will escalate their violence and control. As an ally to your loved one, you may become a target of that person. This may involve emotional and verbal attacks, and even physical violence or threats. Asking questions about how your loved one's partner has responded in the past to outside involvement can help you assess the risk to your loved one and yourself.

Here is a partial list of behaviors to help you identify if the person who chooses violence may escalate over outside help:

- Escalating violence or control after an attempt to leave
- Violence or threats directed at law enforcement
- Involvement in a gang or other organized crime activities
- Assaultive or threatening behavior directed at friends and family who have tried to help
- Continuation or escalation of violence in response to an intervention order or arrest

The partner's status in the community, connections to law enforcement or other forms of privilege may mean they feel like they can act with impunity. The presence of any of these factors means great caution needs to be taken when helping out your loved one.

ALLY BEHAVIOR #3: TELL THEM ALL THE THINGS THAT THEY ARE DOING RIGHT!

The Why: People who choose violence and coercive control blame the survivor for what he is doing to them. Attacks on character and behavior are regular parts of these patterns. At the same time, survivors are often managing to keep jobs, maintain relationships, parent children and work hard to make the relationship work with their partner. Your loved one's sense of self and ability to plan for safety is increased when you validate the things she is doing right. Your validation can go a long way to break the mental control exercised by the person choosing violence.

DOMESTIC VIOLENCE IN DIVERSE SITUATIONS: Across communities, many of us have much higher expectations of women as parents than of men as parents. What this means is you may miss how hard she is working to just keep the children going to school everyday, or getting them to the doctor, or getting the shopping done. In abusive situations, these basic tasks can be much harder to complete. Being a good ally means validating your loved one about how her partner's behaviors have made those basic tasks harder to complete. Tell her how amazing she is for keeping the children on track!

The How: Here is how you validate. Assume she is trying to make a safety plan for herself and her children.

- Even when her choices are hard to understand or different from the ones you might make, assume that her decisions are shaped by the desire for safety, for ending the abuse and trying to do the best by her children.
- Remember that she is often balancing complex needs for herself and for her children. For example, leaving the relationship might mean greater physical and emotional safety but it may mean leaving a school district that is providing good support to her special needs child. Leaving may mean she is homeless and might lose the children to child protection, or to the person choosing violence.
- Remember that some of the formal choices like calling the police, filing for divorce or getting an intervention order may make things worse.

Listen and look for her strengths in coping with the situation and protecting the children. In the following examples we paired opposite actions so you can get a better sense of how her safety strategies may vary depending on his pattern:

- Keeping a job despite his efforts to sabotage her work
- Quitting her job so he doesn't target her co-workers
- Getting an intervention order to keep him away from her
- Not getting an intervention order so as not to escalate the violence
- Pretending to friends that nothing is wrong so he doesn't punish her for talking to others
- Telling her friends about his abuse so they can provide support
- Working hard to placate him so that he doesn't become abusive to her
- Confronting him on his behavior so that she has the sense that she is sticking up for herself
- Sending children to their room to prevent them from seeing his violence
- Keeping the children close to her so that she can better monitor their safety
- Taking children to a refuge/shelter so they are physically safe
- Not taking the children to refuge so they can stay in a familiar environment
- Taking children to a therapist for help
- Keep children from a therapist because it might escalate his violence
- Putting herself between him and the children to protect them
- Punishing the children so he won't punish them worse
- Reading to her children every night before bed to comfort them
- Focusing on the person who chooses violence at night so the children can go to sleep peacefully
- Giving her family extensive access to the children so they can support them
- Keeping the children from her family because he acts worse when her family is involved
- Taking the children to their regular medical appointments so they are cared for
- Keeping them from medical professionals because he doesn't want the abuse disclosed
- Moving the children repeatedly to try to keep them safe
- Staying in one place with the abuser to try to keep the children near friends and family
- Maintaining the household so the children have a normal routine
- Neglecting household tasks because he's constantly criticizing her for doing everything wrong

> **!** **Action:** Every survivor has developed strategies for resisting or overcoming coercive control. In order to see the strengths of your loved one, you need to keep an open mind and resist judgments.

Once you have identified all the things she's doing right, validate her using the following types of statements:

- *"I see how hard you have been working to make things better/keep yourself and your children safe in the face of your partner's behavior."*
- *"I see how hard you've been working to keep the kids on track with school, doctor's appointments, etc."*
- *"It must be hard to not tell the truth about what has been happening. I don't blame you for hiding it from me."*
- *"I see how hard you've been working to make the relationship work."*
- *"Your children are lucky to have a mom who is focused on their well-being no matter what."*

> **HELPING YOUR LOVED ONE SAFELY:** Friends and family may need to call law enforcement, get an intervention order that protects them, or reach out for their own supports if they become the target of the person who chooses violence.

ALLY BEHAVIOR #4: OFFER PRACTICAL SUPPORT.

The Why: Practical support can help improve your loved one's situation. It comes in many forms depending on the person's pattern who chooses violence, your loved one's hopes and fears, the practical situation and resources, and your willingness and ability to help. Your assistance, at whatever level and whatever form, can really make a difference in the physical and emotional health and safety of your loved one and her children.

The How: Start by addressing your concerns for her and the children's safety and well-being, and expressing your desire to help.

- *"Given that you've seen no change in his pattern, I remain concerned for you and your children. What can I do to help?"*
- *"You've been trying to make this work for so long but unless he makes a decision to change, I don't think he is going to get better. How can I help you be in a better situation?"*

The best way to help is to collaboratively plan with your loved one. This means asking her the following questions:

- What can I do to make things better?
- How can I help you create more safety for yourself and your children?
- How can I help you when you are afraid or feel in danger?
- How can you feel connected to your children/your partner while being safe?
- How can I support you as you navigate the abuse you are experiencing?
- How can I help you be safer?
- Who else knows about your situation?
- Who else can we safely involve?
- How can I help you feel more supported?
- What are your biggest fears?

> **Action:** Tell her these things over and over again. You can't validate too much.

You can also prepare for collaboratively planning together by reflecting on what you are willing and able to do:
- Are you willing and able to provide emotional support through listening and validation?
- Are you willing and able to provide concrete practical support like:
  - Drive her to appointments?
  - Lend her your car so she can go to see a lawyer or court?
  - Provide financial assistance so she can pay a security deposit on an apartment?
  - Let her stay at your house while she is in the process of leaving?
  - Talk to the person who chooses violence about his behavior?
  - Provide support and comfort for her children?
  - Take care of the children so they can spend more time in a safe environment and your loved one has some respite from caring for them, or can take steps to get ready to leave or seek help?
  - Keep documents and papers so they are safe for when she needs them?
  - Keep written record of what she is telling you and what you have seen so you can be a more powerful witness in court related to custody and access?

DOMESTIC VIOLENCE IN DIVERSE SITUATIONS: If religion, culture, or connection to the land is very important to your loved one, then you can best help by asking things like, "How can I help you be safer and remain connected to your culture?"

LISTENING TO THE VOICES OF CHILDREN: Children need special attention in these situations. They need safety first and foremost. And they also need someone to listen to their feelings, which are often confusing for them. They may be worried about their mother's safety and also angry at her for not leaving. They may be scared of the person who chooses violence but also love them. As an ally, listen to their ambivalence and confusion. Help them sort through their own feelings. Remind them it's okay to love the person who is choosing violence and to want them to stop hurting people.

Other steps you can take:

Educate yourself about local refuge and support resources for survivors of violence and coercive control. Even if your loved one isn't ready to access those services herself or can't safely access them even by phone, you can provide her with information. Talking to those services can help you as well.

Talk to a lawyer about your loved one's options related to divorce, custody, and access. The more informed you are, the more you can provide educated guidance.

Any or all of these choices to help come with some level of risk for yourself and your loved one. As a friend or a family member, you need to decide what you are willing and able to do. You need to listen to your loved one and follow their wishes as much as possible. They will have the best sense of their partner's reactions. You can plan and create agreements about code words, needs and supports in emergency situations or during heightened times of stress.

HELPING YOUR LOVED ONE SAFELY: What if you don't agree with her decisions? The toughest decisions are the ones where you may need to take action even if the survivor is afraid of the consequences. Just be aware that if you call the police - even when the survivor doesn't want to - you may be doing something that escalates the danger. You need to balance your need to act with their wishes and guidance.

SECTION 7:
Getting your own help and other issues

HAVING A LOVED ONE WHO IS ABUSED IS HARD AND SCARY.

It is painful and traumatizing to watch a loved one being abused. It is natural to feel fearful, frustrated, angry and confused - especially if there are children involved. Often, because we are afraid, we want to convince or force the person being abused to leave. This may or may not be the best choice for your loved one. Being an ally means listening to her understanding of the situation and following her lead.

> **HELPING YOUR LOVED ONE SAFELY:** Child welfare involvement can be one of the scariest moments for your loved one. Survivors often report they are more afraid of child welfare taking their children than they are of their partner's abuse. At the same time, child welfare's involvement can be helpful or it can lead to an escalation in abuse. As a close person to your loved one, child welfare may reach out to you for information, to be part of family meetings or even care for the children. Try to remain in collaboration with your loved one every step along the way. Remember to share your concerns about the abuse in a manner that communicates the following: the actions of the person choosing violence, how those actions have affected your loved one and their children, and your loved one's efforts to protect the children.

Despite your best efforts to be an ally, your loved one may not be willing or able to talk to you about the abuse. As a best friend, sibling or parent, you may be confused about why your loved one isn't sharing their situation. Try to be understanding about the reasons why she doesn't feel ready or safe to talk more openly. In some instances, the survivor is trying to protect the family. For example, if she believes that a family member will confront the person who is choosing to be violent and that someone may get hurt, she may not disclose. Disclosure is a big step and often feels like a scary loss of control for the survivor - "If I tell someone, I don't know what will happen next. Will things get worse?" Do everything you can to communicate to the survivor your desire to be her ally, which means, as best you can, honor her wishes.

You may also be afraid that if you raise issues of abuse you will be "cut off" from your loved one, particularly the children. Only you can decide the trade-offs and risks. Try to remember that these types of actions are likely being done out of fear, self-protection and possibly protection of you. Your loved one may be fearful that contact will escalate the abuse or feel shame for their situation. Keeping contact with the survivor, giving them general support and connection, particularly staying close to the children may be the only thing you can do. This may be a lot in the situation. Continue to tell the survivor that they deserve to be happy, and that they are worthy of love and respectful treatment. You can also be a place of physical and emotional safety for the children. These experiences may not feel like enough now but they may matter in the long run.

As an ally to a loved one who is being abused, you need and deserve support. This may mean leaning on other allies who are aware of the situation or reaching out for professional assistance. Support can help you manage your fears and feelings of powerlessness. Getting your own support can make you a better ally.

WHAT ABOUT OUR RELATIONSHIP WITH THE PERSON WHO CHOOSES VIOLENCE?

The person who chooses violence or control may be someone who is related to us or we care about. It may be our son, son-in-law, uncle, father or other kin. In some cases, it will be hard to believe that they've been acting abusively. In other instances, it may not be any sort of surprise. Be careful not to be drawn into the person who is using violence's justifications or excuses for his violent behavior. You can still care about him while still believing the survivor and being her ally.

You need to be prepared to keep the information that your loved one shares with you in complete confidence. This may mean acting like you do not know the things you know. This may be hard, but may be very necessary. As an ally, keeping your loved one's confidence, and not letting the person choosing violence know that you know about the abuse, may be the most important and hardest thing you do.

In instances where your loved one feels like it may help, you may be able to talk to the person who chooses violence about their behaviors. If you are an important person to him, your opinion about his behavior may be influential. You may be able to communicate to him that his behavior is unacceptable, and you worry about the effects of his behaviors on their family members. You can also express your worry about his behavior harming his relationships with his partner and his children.

In each situation, you will need to assess whether talking to this person about their behavior is safe for you and for the survivor. This is especially true if the person who is choosing violence will be angry at their partner for talking to you. Here are some things to consider if you want to talk to the person who chooses violence about his behavior:

- Do not betray the confidence and trust of the survivor. Discuss with her the idea of you talking to the person who chooses violence about his behavior. Determine together if this is a safe choice for you and her. Figure out how you can talk about the situation. Decide with the survivor if you can share whether you've been talking to her or not. Respect her boundaries.
- Assess your relationship with the person who uses violence. Does this person respect your opinion? Does he have a history of violence with others besides his partners? Consider whether a direct or indirect approach is best. An indirect approach might involve checking in on his relationships with his partner and children, and involves only talking about things you have directly observed. The more direct approach might be to talk to him about how he is handling his anger and stress. The most direct approach involves direct discussion of control and abuse.
- Check in with the survivor after you have your discussion with the person who chooses violence to see if it had any negative repercussions for her.

WHAT IF I HAVE PROBLEMS WITH THE SURVIVOR'S BEHAVIOR?

Domestic violence survivors are human, like anyone else. They might be a difficult person, use drugs, be impacted by depression, or be a poor parent. Maybe they cheated on their partner. They might have been verbally abusive to their children, partner, or even you. It is important to remember that flawed behavior by the survivor doesn't excuse coercive control or violence. It is still her partner's choice about how they act. Sometimes we want to say, "They are both messed up." If you want to help your loved one, you need to be clear that even difficult behaviors, like using drugs, don't justify violence or coercive control.

It's important to remember that some of these difficult behaviors may be a direct result of being abused. For example, your loved one may have started drinking more to self medicate to deal with being abused. Your loved one's drinking problem doesn't excuse anyone being violent toward her.

The survivor's trauma responses may not be comfortable for you. She may get angry with you for trying to help because the help feels scary. Try to understand what might be behind the anger, draw the boundaries you need to, and keep reminding the survivor that you are there for them and they don't deserve to be abused.

Your loved one may be suspicious of others - including you - even when you are trying to help them. Remember that the person who chooses abuse has made it harder for them to trust others and may have used others to spy on them.

WHAT'S THE ROLE OF ALCOHOL AND OTHER DRUGS IN MY LOVED ONE'S SITUATION?

Alcohol or other drugs do not cause someone to be violent or controlling. This is a separate issue. Some people are more violent when they drink or use drugs. Others may use control and violence to protect and support their drug use. For example, someone may use threats of violence to get his partner to give him money to do drugs, or to pressure her to use substances with him. Even though substance use and coercive control are two separate problems, getting help for substances is always a good idea. It will help the person choosing violence to think more clearly, may reduce levels of control and violence and reduce the family's fear levels.

If your loved one is involved with substance misuse, they are likely to benefit from support and assistance. That said, feeling physically and emotionally safe will make her efforts easier and more likely to succeed. If she feels safe, she may no longer feel the desire to use substances. Any effort to get her help must consider whether her partner will try to sabotage those efforts. As an ally, you can help plan how to get help as safely as possible. This may mean driving her to appointments or watching the children so she doesn't have to depend on her partner for childcare.

MY LOVED ONE HOLDS RELIGIOUS OR OTHER STRONGLY HELD BELIEFS ABOUT MARRIAGE, FAMILY AND RELATIONSHIPS.

Survivors often have deeply held religious beliefs about the sacredness of marriage. They may also hold other beliefs about family and marriage. A common one is that children need to have a father. These values and beliefs are deeply personal and need to be respected by those trying to help them. As an ally, you can explore these beliefs with your loved one. One approach is to talk about how their partner's choice to be violent is a violation of the sacredness of marriage and household peace. You can also validate her desire to have a father in their children's lives but also ask questions about what kind of role model he is being for the children. Asking, "How can I help you be safer and more nurtured while you live and honor the principles of your religious beliefs?" is a very important question. You can also ask, "What needs to shift in your partner so that he can be a better, safer parent?" Expecting that a victim suddenly casts aside a deeply held religious belief or her desire for her children to have a father is not an effective strategy.

I'M WORRIED MY MALE FAMILY MEMBER IS BEING ABUSED BY HIS FEMALE PARTNER.
Women can be abusive and controlling toward a male partner. Women can even commit acts of physical violence toward male partners. These behaviors can be emotionally harmful but much less frequently involve physical injury or fear. Coercive control is much less prevalent even when a woman chooses to use violence. When a male has their own trauma history, has a disability or other factors that make them more vulnerable, they may experience coercive control. Unfortunately, it can be hard to sort out which males are true victims, and which are males who choose to use coercive control but choose to present themselves as victims. These persons make it harder for true male victims to be identified because they are manipulating others by leaving out part of the story or making complete lies about their partner's use of violence. You can use the questions outlined earlier in this guide to help you figure out the situation.

[*Do you have a male loved one who you are afraid of being abused? Learn about the resources in your local area for male abuse survivors.*]

CAN PERSONS WHO CHOOSE VIOLENCE STOP THOSE BEHAVIORS?
The short answer is yes. The longer answer is, it takes a lot of work and commitment. This type of change is often long and slow, and often needs outside professional support. In many locations, there are men's behavior change programs that can be a resource for someone who wants to change. Often persons who choose violence are resistant to getting help and need to suffer some loss or consequence before they seek help. An arrest or a partner leaving can be a catalyst for change.

Survivors often hope that their partner will change. This is a very reasonable desire. Being an ally, you can help them make a realistic assessment of change. Change is much more than promises or apologies. Here are three common-sense questions you can ask your loved one when she talks about her hopes that her partner has changed:
- Has her partner admitted to a meaningful portion of what he has done? ('Naming the behaviors')
- Is he able to talk about the impact of his abusive behaviors on himself and others? ('Claiming the harm')
- What changes has he made in his behavior pattern? ('Making real changes')

The last item, behavior change, is the most important. Part of coercive control can involve claiming he has changed to convince your loved one to stop legal action or to take him back. Coercive control and violence are violations of trust. The person who has chosen violence may never be able to restore that trust. A good ally will support their loved one that she is under no obligation to trust her partner ever again or to take him back even when he promises to change. Persons who choose violence need to accept their lack of control over those decisions by your loved one. If the person who chooses violence is really committed to change, they will pursue it whether their partner comes back to them or not. Real change is demonstrated over time, through consistent, new behavior - especially in circumstances where, in the past, he would've chosen violence or control. For example, if in the past he would've prevented her from working outside the home through verbal abuse and stalking, one measure of change would be that she could freely work outside the home without the fear of punishment.

Resources

INTERNATIONAL SURVIVOR RESOURCES

To support allies of survivors, here are some national-level support contacts. Most of the phone numbers are a mixture of 24-hour-a-day hotlines and business-hour helpline services. Many provide online chat services as well. The services provided by these agencies are generally free. All phone numbers are local to that country. Many of these agencies also offer support and referrals for male survivors of domestic violence.

(Australia) National sexual assault, domestic and family violence counselling service:
　　　　https://1800Respect.org.au Ph: 1800 737 732
(Australia) Lifeline: https://www.lifeline.org.au/ Ph: 13 11 14
(Australia) Men's Line: https://mensline.org.au/ Ph: 1300 78 99 78
(Australia) Kids Helpline: https://kidshelpline.com.au/ Ph: 1800 55 1800
(Canada) Shelter Safe: https://www.sheltersafe.ca/
　　　　(provides a list of domestic abuse shelters in each province and territory with phone numbers)
(Hong Kong) Hong Kong Federation of Women's Centres: https://womencentre.org.hk/ Ph: 2386 6255
(New Zealand) Women's Refuge: https://womensrefuge.org.nz/ Ph: 0800 REFUGE or 0800 733 843
(New Zealand) It's Not Ok Campaign: http://www.areyouok.org.nz/ Ph: 0800 456 450
(New Zealand) Lifeline: https://www.lifeline.org.nz/ Ph: 0800 543 354
(Northern Ireland) Northern Ireland Women's Aid: https://www.womensaidni.org/ Ph: 0808 802 1414
(Scotland) Scottish Women's Aid: https://womensaid.scot/ Ph: 0800 027 1234
(Singapore) Association of Women for Action and Research: https://www.aware.org.sg/ Ph: 1800 777 5555
(UK) National Domestic Abuse Helpline: https://www.nationaldahelpline.org.uk/ Ph: 0808 2000 247
(UK) National LGBT+ Domestic Abuse Helpline: http://www.galop.org.uk/domesticabuse/
　　　　Ph: 0800 999 5428
(UK) Respect Men's Advice Line: https://mensadviceline.org.uk/ Ph: 0808 8010327
(US) National Domestic Violence Hotline: https://thehotline.org Ph: 1-800-799-7233/1-800-787-3224 (TTY)
(US) StrongHearts Native Helpline: https://www.strongheartshelpline.org/ Ph: 1-844-762-8483
(US) The National Deaf Domestic Violence Hotline: https://thedeafhotline.org/
　　　　Videophone: 1-855-812-1001
(Wales) Welsh Women's Aid: https://www.welshwomensaid.org.uk/ Ph: 0808 80 10 800

ADDITIONAL RESOURCES

Technology can help provide safe communication with your loved ones, or it can be a way for the person using violence to monitor and stalk your loved one's communication and movements. This website, www.techsafety.org, sponsored by the US-based National Network to End Domestic Violence, is a resource about technology and abuse for allies and their loved ones, and how to safely use technology to communicate.

Notes

Notes

www.ingramcontent.com/pod-product-compliance
Lightning Source LLC
Chambersburg PA
CBHW041659040426
42444CB00021B/3479